TRAINING IN NO TIME

With a well-trained dog, you will never return home to a scene like this.

TRAINING
IN NO TIME

**An Expert's Approach
to Effective Dog Training
for Hectic Life Styles**

AMY AMMEN

Photographs by Jan Plagenz

Illustrations by Michelle Juergens

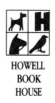

HOWELL
BOOK
HOUSE

Macmillan General Reference
A Simon & Schuster Macmillan Company
1633 Broadway
New York, NY 10019

Library of Congress Cataloging-in-Publication Data
Ammen, Amy
   Training in no time : an expert's approach to effective dog training for hectic life styles
/ by Amy Ammen; photos by Jan Plagenz; illustrations by Michelle Juergens.
   p. cm.
   ISBN 0-87605-778-4
   1. Includes index. 2. Dogs—Training. 3. Dogs—behavior.
I. Title.
SF431.A44 1995
636.7'0887—dc20 94-37151
   CIP
Manufactured in the United States of America
10   9   8

Dedicated to the memories of
William R. Koehler, Job Michael Evans
and Barbara Goodman,
and to their expertise
and unfailing willingness to share it.

During training, it is often helpful to use a cable, lead or similar link in the home to be able to get to a dog without having to lunge for him. And, it's a fact, a dog knows when it must listen.

CONTENTS

There are many sides to a well-trained dog. If your pet is perfectly house-trained but goes through your garbage can like a preschooler through a toy chest, you need to go back to the drawing board.

INTRODUCTION

Thanks to my friend, Jacqueline Fraser, a misconception about me prevails. In the introduction of *Dual Ring Dog*, a book we coauthored, Jackie claimed I was blessed with grace and natural dog-training ability. Although I was initially proud that I fooled her, I have been haunted by that perception since. At the seminars I present to dog obedience trial competitors nationwide, doubters and insecure types believe only the gifted can duplicate my success.

While it's true that I began training at age 11, I owe my career to my initial ineffectiveness. You see, I attended my first obedience class out of desperation. I spent three months, four hours per week attending a beginners class with my first dog, Tess, a nine-month-old Siberian Husky. Unfortunately, upon completion, Tess was still digging, jumping, running away, biting and house soiling. To continue classes, I was forced to become a member of the sponsoring club and to pay for training by the year. Thanks to the encouragement of some fellow club members, 80 more hours of class and as much practice at home, I entered my first obedience competition. After all that preparation, Tess and I demonstrated exactly how disconnected a team could be while still attached by a leash.

In spite of my rocky beginnings, five years later I began instructing obedience classes. Seventeen students were enrolled in my first class; only one remained for graduation. Although by this time I was a successful trainer, and my dogs, including the Husky, achieved impressive wins, obviously I couldn't instruct humans. But I didn't stop trying, and today my instructors and I give lessons to hundreds of students per week through Amiable Dog Training School in Milwaukee.

Although never academically, athletically or socially inclined, I loved my dogs and was absorbed by them. I was 18 years old and had devoted seven all-consuming years to learning about dogs when Jackie and I met.

So when Jackie—who, by the way, has the greatest zest for life and an uncanny mastery of vast and diverse talents—calls me a natural, I'm inclined to protest. Ironically, in the introduction of *Dual Ring Dog,* Jackie, the horseback riding, deep-sea diving diva, presents herself as uncoordinated and clumsy.

Why do perfectly capable individuals deny their own accomplishments? To boast after arguing against our potential would be admitting we underestimate our capabilities. All of us—Jackie, you and I—have infinite potential waiting to be recognized.

Feeling like a failure while pursuing goals is typical. Don't use it as an excuse to give up. Everyone does have the ability to be a successful dog trainer in a fraction of the time it took Jackie and me to learn. Before you turn this page, acknowledge that you physically and mentally possess the makings of an outstanding dog trainer. Now that you've freed your mind from limitations, sit back, read and let nature take its course.

ACKNOWLEDGMENTS

My thanks to Jan Plagenz, Sandy Plagenz, Michelle Juergens, Bryan Garness, Nancy Garness, Kitty Foth and Lisa Moy. I needed your support in so many ways. None of you have ever let me down. I'll always be grateful, and I hope to be able to return the kindness, to all of you, my steadfast friends.

Also thanks to Elias and Michael and the good staff at The Cafe Knickerbocker, for allowing me to work on this manuscript hour after hour, for weeks on end, in "The Classiest Cafe in the World."

Of course, thanks to my students for testing the validity of these methods and to the staff of Amiable Dog Training for making me look good when I had other obligations: Ed Bower, Denise Elger, Nancy Luecke, Ed Muraczewski, Patti Muraczewski, Bobbie Oxley, Patti Richards and Mary Steckle.

The children in the photographs—Alan, Elaine, Jennie and Robert Carsky—were perfect and so cooperative. When the kids become famous, Jan and Sandy Plagenz want everyone to know that they discovered them.

TRAINING IN NO TIME

Using daily, subtle clues to instill good habits results in consistent, socially acceptable behavior under all normal circumstances for the well-trained companion dog.

CHAPTER 1

Deliver a Big Message
with Little Signals

A re you looking for the magic cure for a nasty habit? Here's the secret: it's not one trick, harsh scolding or final beating that will correct a problem. Sure, occasionally an owner will do something just once and the dog will never misbehave again. I once heard of an owner attaching air-filled balloons to a door to stop her dog from scratching when she left the house. She returned to find a mass of popped balloons and the scratching never occurred again. Although this dog's bad habit has been successfully corrected, many other dogs might be temporarily frightened by the popping balloons but will continue scratching when the balloons are not in place. Often even worse behavior emerges, like excessive barking, destroying valuables or clawing woodwork, upholstery or drapery, to relieve the frustration of being left alone.

When seeking solutions to behavioral problems, owners are often advised to neuter, give more exercise or obedience train. While these are important components of an overall program, neutering doesn't teach a dog to come or stay clean indoors, exercising by itself will only give the dog more stamina for naughtiness, and practicing obedience routines in the backyard has little effect on house manners.

The surest way to get permanent, positive results is to recognize and change the few big ambiguities that allowed problems to surface and to use daily, subtle cues to instill, not destroy, good habits.

DISCOVERING THE CORE OF UNWANTED BEHAVIOR

Several years ago, an experienced obedience trial trainer attended my basic obedience class with her young Bouvier des Flandres. Brenda built a good foundation of control and was a diligent student. We kept in touch after the course, so I knew competitive training was progressing well, but apart from formal training sessions, Griz was untrustworthy off leash. Discouraged by "experts" who claimed Bouviers must always be leashed, Brenda became convinced Griz would never enjoy galloping freely as her older Collie does on their daily hikes through rural pastures. I reassured Brenda that no breed had a patent on problems and suggested ignoring trainers who would rather look for excuses than for solutions. After questioning Brenda about her techniques, I recommended some changes, but it wasn't until Brenda invited me to a dinner party that I confirmed my suspicions: Griz "practiced" commands, but had no manners.

Pulling into the driveway, Brenda's spouse, Greg, shouted parking instructions over Griz's barking. Since Griz's cable enabled him to run into my parking spot, Greg held Griz's collar as he warned me about the exuberant greeting I was about to receive. Sure enough, after Greg talked and stroked Griz until he was no longer hyperventilating, Greg released the collar and Griz now welcomed me with uninvited jumps, sniffs, dancing and kisses.

As guests gathered in the small kitchen, Brenda crated Griz to get him out of the way. Griz, still excited and not finished with his hellos, barked loudly. Brenda's and Greg's intermittent attempts to hush Griz were ignored. Once most of the guests had moved into the living room, Brenda released Griz in the kitchen and began food preparations. I offered to help and watched, speechless, as Griz's counter-level nose conveniently scanned every morsel. Griz obliged Brenda's meek effort to shoo him from the area by moseying down to another part of the long counter.

Instead of coping with Griz's troublesome manners, Brenda and Greg could have made the evening a positive experience for Griz and their guests alike. As gracious, attentive hosts, Brenda and Greg focused their attention on their guests and unknowingly sabotaged their off-leash control. Griz was allowed to lead a double life of performing short obedience routines in practice and doing whatever he pleased without interference the rest of the time. Swiftly enforcing the stay command as we drove up and correcting excessive barking, inappropriate sniffing of guests and jumping could have been a marvelous reinforcement of the respect and rapport built during obedience lessons. Had Griz's owners used "sneakaways" (described in chapter 5) to control him as the first guests arrived, the big, lovable dog would have been on his best behavior the entire evening.

Toxic Training

Unmanageable or polished, all dogs are "trained" and conditioned to respond as they do. Whether we approve or disapprove, our dog's

There is no quicker way to sabotage good training than to tolerate your dog's pulling.

behavior is being molded 24 hours a day. Dogs are among the most observant creatures, and there's a reason for everything they do. Human oversights, inconsistencies, miscommunications and contradictions teach dogs "inappropriate" behavior. From the dog's point of view, he is simply coping, surviving and existing in a confused environment the best he can.

If nothing is working, you may be too close to the problem and blind to the obvious. If you truly want a solution, ask an outsider to expose the poison in your program.

Strategy

Training in No Time is the simplest, most efficient way to permanently foster a healthy pet and owner relationship. To map out a strategy:

1. Decide what you want. Your goal may be to stop Pebbles from using the house as a toilet. Vow to love her unconditionally, but refuse to accept misbehavior, and commit to using every humane measure necessary to stop it.

2. Recognize inconsistency. Address any situation in which you feel powerless. Does the thought of vacationing with your dog create visions of barking, jumping, whining or soiling? Are there things you avoid or can't do with your pet?

   If your main concern is house soiling, walking manners may seem irrelevant, but straining at the end of the leash should be treated as a power struggle and stopped. Profound changes often occur only after making lots of small but significant changes. An otherwise finely tuned car won't start if one of its spark plugs isn't engaging. Fixing the missing connections that short out good training are often just as simple.

3. Plan and implement changes using the suggestions in this book.

Whether you are losing, gaining or maintaining weight, a diet is what you eat, be it carrots or fudge. Similarly, training isn't what you try to teach; it's what your dog learns, good or bad.

CHAPTER 2

Quality Versus Quantity

et's get the facts straight:

There are 24 hours in everyone's day. Good trainers definitely don't work harder or longer, they work smarter.

Even perfectly trained dogs require attention, love, and time for feeding, cleanup and exercise. Determine the minimum amount of time necessary for attending to his basic needs and be loyal to that commitment. No matter how busy they are, devoted owners always provide good care and hire outside help when necessary.

Even the dumbest dogs learn every moment. They know what makes them comfortable, happy, anxious and fearful. Smart trainers take note so they can trigger a desired response in an instant.

Dog training happens fast, and dogs have incredible memories. How long does it take a dog to learn that the perfect time to raid the garbage is when his master is talking on the phone or getting ready for work, or that if he steals a sock during an engrossing television show, he suddenly has the family's undivided attention? It is easy to teach good behavior instantly and simply if we have the right temperament. Note that the dog's success depends on our attitude, not his.

Dynamite Training Attitude

Positive TNT (Training in No Time) can explode with every interaction. You don't have to be a natural to have a "way with dogs." We all can consciously contract the "knack."

7

Visualize a well-trained dog, and that will be the only kind you will ever want.

Develop acute sensitivity

Be aware of how present actions influence future behavior. Laughing as your pup drags you across the park to greet another household member encourages the dog to jubilantly bound at other people and dogs who may prefer fighting to flirting. Suppressing natural impulses is often neccessary to protect the dog's safety.

Don't be patient

Stop hoping that time and maturity will take the place of training. Puppyhood is temporary, but bad habits last a lifetime. Determine what you'd like to change about your dog's behavior now, and take the necessary steps that will bring about those changes.

Find a role model

Do you know a really well-trained dog? Visualize what it would be like to own him. Expect a change in behavior for the better in your dog, and you will naturally begin fostering the right code of behavior.

Look for opportunities in misbehavior

Maybe your dog is disruptive during car rides. While it is necessary to drive him to the veterinarian, groomer and kennel, you'd also enjoy including him on trips and when running errands. Instead of training in the backyard, work on your dog's cruise control on the back road. Put learning in high gear by getting control where it is most needed. Dogs become noticeably content immediately following sensible enforcement and are far easier to control in totally different situations as a result.

Admit mistakes

Whiners pass blame on to their dog. Instead of cursing the food-stealing canine, successful trainers place blame for wrongdoing on themselves. They understand that somewhere along the line they allowed the dog the opportunity to learn the misbehavior. Griping about the problem is a waste of time and energy, unless it provides incentive to follow problem-solving strategies.

Find ways to control situations you've been avoiding

Walk past Brutus's house, and control your dog when he shows more interest in his buddy than in you. Although you may not get around the block, you'll stimulate his mind, refresh and relax him and enjoy the bonding that results from better understanding.

Temporarily eliminate problems you don't have the focus to control

Trainers of multiple dogs will sometimes tell one to "stay" while they work another. As the handler gives his undivided attention to the dog being taught intricate obedience exercises, he can't be aware of what the other is doing. This misuse of obedience breaks the most basic rule: Always be prepared to correct. It's much smarter to tie the dog and

Consider how difficult life with an untrained or poorly trained dog can be, and you will be sure to make your dog the well-behaved pet you have always wanted.

improve the stay by practicing around casual, understanding guests, when the exercise is most difficult and most valuable.

The "cross your fingers" method of training is popular around the house, too. Dog owners give commands because they want to keep the dog out of the way, knowing they lack the focus to enforce it should the dog lack the reliability to follow the order. Countless times dog owners have wondered aloud why their dog is selectively obedient. Often they give a sit command, and if the dog is moving but still reasonably controlled, they figure he is behaving acceptably. I listen, amazed that they have no idea of the disobedience they've just taught.

Obedience For Your Convenience

Busy dog owners can't afford the inconvenience of an untrained dog. Chasing runaway dogs, losing sleep because of a noisy dog and working extra hours to pay for destruction will unnecessarily chew up free time. Save sanity by devoting a fraction of that time to learning about dog behavior and anticipating goofs. Enlightened owners are aware of what allows a good dog to learn bad things.

Although there is never enough time to do everything, there is always enough time to do the important things. Grab opportunities during routine interactions to teach your dog all he needs to know. Use grooming time, daily walks, car rides and visiting guests as occasions to improve your dog's behavior.

CHAPTER 3

Compassionately Connected

J ennifer joined a dog-training class with her lively, noisy nine-month-old Bichon/Poodle-mix, Calvin. Tightly matted hair surrounding his ears, an indication of benign neglect, was easily seen as Jennifer held him throughout class. Since he was small enough to pick up and carry, Jennifer figured she didn't need to train Calvin to remain still or walk nicely.

The following week she returned to class with her now shaved, yapping, pulling puppy. She didn't use any of the previous week's tips to control him. Since the class always began with a review and demonstration of the previous week's lesson, the instructor hoped Jennifer was eager to catch up. Two handlers successfully demonstrated the "no pulling exercise," and Jennifer was next. Attempts to verbalize key elements were lost on Jennifer, whose technique was less than effective. The empathic teacher asked Jennifer if she would like a brief demonstration. After a minute of practice with the instructor, Calvin was happily attentive. However, Jennifer was upset. Not because Calvin couldn't learn; with the right techniques he proved to be an eager student. Not because she didn't know how to teach; the members of the class demonstrated how simple it was. Jennifer was bound to be disappointed because she expected Calvin to listen, just because he was a dog, rather than because of proper training. Like the owner of a plane, expecting it to fly without a pilot, Jennifer must realize Calvin will reach his potential only when she assumes her role as pilot.

Although Jennifer thought it might be nice to have a dog that would walk nicely, allow her to brush his hair, be quiet when necessary and come when called, the price of requiring him to consider her requests more important than his impulses was too high.

Many well-intentioned owners believe dogs are meant to be free spirits, indulged and pacified. Dogs suffer needless anxiety and confusion and, often, death at the hands of wish-granting genies. Countless runaways are killed in accidents, biters get put to sleep and owners surrender dogs to the humane society, saying, "I wish I could keep him but I'm moving," as they euphemistically believe the problems they've nurtured will miraculously disappear in the new home.

Lovingly Denied

Catering to your dog's every whim will not only threaten his safety, it will also stunt his character. Many dogs are encouraged to behave like a baby who is crowned emperor—empowered but oblivious to the consequences of his decisions. Remember, dogs are pack animals and have a work ethic and a curiosity that, if not controlled, can lead to behaviors that ultimately can cost them their lives. If you truly cherish your dog, indulge him with leadership, understanding and direction. Enrich your dog's life by depriving him of that which teaches ill manners.

He's So Cute, He's Annoying

Many annoying habits begin as adorable traits or useful signals that we are happy to acknowledge. Before we realize the real message we've sent, an awful characteristic has taken root. Innocently tossing the pup a tidbit when he glances at our meal encourages begging. Soon every time food is near he'll stare longingly, drool at our knee, bark, nudge or even steal, growl and bite to get and keep the food to which he feels he's entitled.

Clever dogs quickly turn kindly owners into automatic door attendants. It begins when the unnecessarily cautious caretaker jumps up to let the dog out each time he meanders past the door, just in case Fido needs to relieve himself (no matter how recent his last outing).

Now he demands to be let out whenever you relax instead of when he needs to go, and because of frequent unnecessary outings, this reduces his capacity to control his bladder and bowels. What a neat way to get your undivided attention!

Remember how that adorable little wet nose used to bashfully nuzzle your hand for a moment just to thank you for being such a good new owner? Naturally, those gentle eyes always melted your heart and brought you to your knees for a full-fledged embrace. Who would have

Many of our dogs' bad habits are fixed in puppyhood and by accident. Begging at the dinner table, inappropriate barking, destructiveness and aggression are examples of what we can teach a dog without realizing we are doing it.

imagined a tyrant lurked within, ready to ambush? With military authority, he storms in every time he hears the page of a newspaper turn and boldly shoves the arm of the unsuspecting reader.

Have you lost your bed to a cover-stealing, space-hogging canine? Does he stop at every tree as you obediently trail behind? Does your canine Mrs. Kravitz consider nothing off limits? Does she invade the privacy of family and guests by barging through partially closed doors, nosing through belongings and unabashedly meddling in every detail?

Some people buy a dog as a distraction from day-to-day work. Even so, use opportunities when you have the dog's full attention to utilize his work ethic and to bond, rather than to indulge his obnoxious tendencies.

When he nudges, take your hand away, then look in his eyes and smile. Then give a command, congratulate (whether he did it on his own or needed help), and once he does it to your satisfaction, release and play a bit before making another request. He'll be proud you've recognized his cleverness, and when you turn your attention back to the matter at hand he'll leave rewarded and satisfied by your positive feedback. You'll think so too. Just by rewarding the nudge with a command rather than with petting, food or a walk, you'll reduce other demanding behavior like unnecessary and frequent requests to go out and begging at the table.

Coiffed and Content

Expect your dog to accept grooming without fidgeting or biting. Acclimate him to restraint and examinations by feeling his ears, feet, nails and tail and by looking at his teeth. Use your free hand to hold his collar. If he struggles or turns defensively toward the working hand, jerk the collar sharply as you lightly maintain your grip or position in the area of objection. Should you stop the procedure, your dog will quickly learn to repeat his behavior when he wants you to stop whatever you are doing.

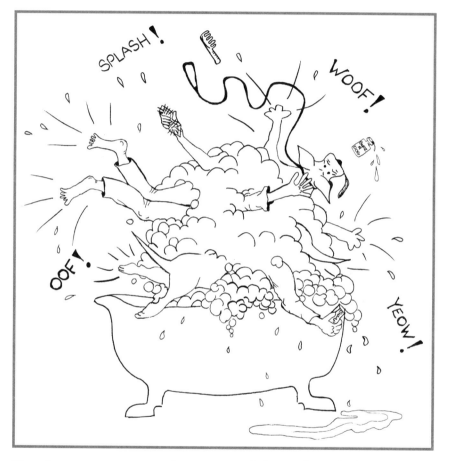

There is never any reason to tolerate resistant behavior during baths or grooming sessions. If you stop what you're doing when your dog struggles, you will show him how to control the situation.

You may want to contact a groomer to learn the proper equipment, brush strokes, manicuring, bathing and teeth- and ear-cleaning procedures. Groom your dog on a platform that measures between waist and calf high on the groomer—the smaller the dog, the taller the platform. You'll be more comfortable and able to see what you're doing. Also, platforms with small surface areas discourage fidgeting. Allow a dancing-footed dog to briefly experience gravity the first time he wiggles. Rescue him a split second after a paw slips off the table, and not only will he respectfully deem you a hero, he also will likely remain contented and happily motionless for future grooming.

Adequately Exercised

Many dog owners are under the mistaken impression their medium-sized or large dogs' need to run will be met by allowing them unsupervised freedom in the backyard. Instead of getting sufficient exercise,

Biking is great exercise for a well-trained dog, but the use of a tight lead is essential to safe biking. With all that slack in his lead, this dog could easily run in front of the bike, causing considerable injury.

boredom prevails, causing the frustrated canine to become destructive or noisy when tied or fenced even in a large area. Hiking in rough terrain, swimming or retrieving for long periods are great exercise options. Expend excess energy by investing 20 or 30 minutes, three to five days a week for vigorous exercise.

If your dog won't retrieve or swim, isn't trustworthy off leash, or is unable to exercise in an open, suitable exercise area, run him on leash by jogging or biking. After teaching wonderful walking manners with sneakaways, jogging and biking will be easy. Before you begin riding, teach him to respect the front tire. Holding the lead tightly in the left hand, keep the dog even with the left pedal or handlebars of the bike while you walk on the right. Steer into him if he forges or interferes with the bike. Begin riding when you're confident your dog won't bolt. For greater stability and balance, buy a "springer" from a pet supply

Dogs are great mirrors of our emotions; if you encourage or praise a frightened dog, he will usually become more fearful.

Ignore the actions of an apprehensive dog and treat him simply as an individual that requires being kept under control.

store. This lightweight bar attaches the dog to the bike so both hands are free to steer.

Scaring Fears Away

Our natural reaction is to console the apprehensive dog. Whether the phobia involves inanimate objects like garbage cans and loud or strange noises, other dogs, children, or places like the veterinarian's office, hallways or stairwells, reassurance only embeds the fear. Ignore his panicky state and force him to concentrate on what he knows best. Teach reliable obedience, and give commands in rapid-fire sequence for two minutes or until he is relaxed or responding automatically to sit, down, stay and come. Then play a bit by running, nudging, patting the ground or talking silly. Continue rapid-fire commands if the dog appears preoccupied by his fear. Practice first in situations in which he's uncomfortable but not panicky, then gradually progress to greater challenges.

If your dog fears going up or down stairs or in or out of an enclosure, leash him and approach him with confidence as you grip the railing and progress up or down one stair at a time, never looking at the dog. Repeat methodically and mechanically until the dog walks with you as he does around the block on leash. When possible, begin with just a few stairs or on a very wide stairway.

Selectively Pampered

No one is suggesting a dog remain curled in a corner unless spoken to, but enforcing requests and setting limitations needn't make you feel guilty. The only things a dog should NEVER be denied are regular feedings, adequate exercise, grooming, veterinary care and a daily playtime which suits your schedule.

"You're No Fun!"

Feeling like a party pooper, a scrooge or a dictator as you enforce the new code of behavior? Since dogs aren't people, how can we expect them to mold to our society and contentedly accept our restrictions? Living under our roof doesn't come naturally, but adhering to pack rules does.

A pup's education begins when he is barely able to walk. Mom instructs with nudges, growls and, when necessary, scruff shakes, bites and pinning to the ground. Lessons include where to relieve itself, when to nurse, and how much rough play is acceptable. Obeying rules, considering pack members' space and receiving discipline for overstepping bounds are a way of life easily understood and accepted by your dog. Now it's your turn to pick up where your dog's mother left off and to understand and accept an authoritative role as a way of life, without guilt.

CHAPTER 4

Fair Play

"Why is he doing this?" the frustrated dog owner asks. If the dog could answer, he'd say that house soiling, jumping, chewing and digging are in his job description. Unfortunately, his owner failed to communicate exactly when and where these actions are acceptable. These are the rules of fair play:

Expect dogs to behave unacceptably at all times, in all places, unless thoroughly instructed otherwise.

Mattie, a five-year-old, obedience trial–winning Australian Shepherd, almost always accompanied Diane, her trainer. On one of their journeys to a new training building, Mattie peacefully strolled around while Diane organized her training equipment. Imagine Diane's surprise when she discovered her supposedly perfectly trained companion had soiled the rug. It is true no harm was done, and the mess was easily cleaned up and forgotten by Diane. But perhaps that experience left an impression on Mattie—obviously she doesn't *always* have to go, when nature calls, outside.

A short time ago I bought BJ, a two-and-a-half-year-old Tibetan Spaniel that was raised within a pack of 20 barking, food-stealing, out-for-their-own-good dogs. I urgently needed to get control of BJ's pack mentality for two reasons: I lived in an apartment where the landlord kindly allowed me to keep dogs in spite of a "no pets" policy, and, as a

Umbilical cording gives you the freedom to train, prevent undesirable behavior, enforce proper manners and attend to your regular household duties all together.

dog trainer, I have a reputation to uphold. With no past history of behavior in my household, new rules were easily set up for BJ, using *Training in No Time* principles.

Two years later, BJ and I arrived at Jan Plagenz's house to shoot the photos for this book. Jan ate lunch as we discussed the choreography. We began gathering equipment, and I noticed BJ perched on the chair, intent on traveling over to Jan's plate via the table top. Instinctively, I leaped across the room to correct. BJ mistakenly assumed tables were off limits only at one Milwaukee address. Since dogs don't always remember their mistakes, in our future visits I'll be more guarded when food is near.

Never play games that encourage misbehavior.

Dogs that display aggressive tendencies in group classes present a potential threat to other class members. Because of safety concerns, aggressive dogs are transferred to private training until the owner can prevent and correct behaviors like lunging and snapping at other dogs, and excessive barking and biting.

Such was the case of Dennis, an adolescent, and his 18-month-old Collie mix, Dillon. After two lessons and tremendous improvement, they returned to the group. As the weeks progressed, Dillon's behavior deteriorated; I attributed it to the familiar learning plateau. It wasn't until the second to the last night of class that the real problem surfaced publicly.

In the "play during training" exercise, handlers play enthusiastically with their dogs to teach instant obedience even when excited. While the other handlers skipped, talked silly, tossed toys and playfully pushed their dogs, Dennis growled, slapped and grabbed the dog's mane of hair in a rolling motion. Naturally, Dillon retaliated by leaping and snapping at his attacker.

Play means fetching, running and patting. Even during nice play, some dogs don't respond in kind. Never deprive your dog of play. Instead, leash him and teach him how to do it properly.

A little abuse is never okay!

Protect your dog from mishandling.

A young couple was buying an adorable Bichon at a pet shop for their two year old. I watched the pup frolic around the shop as they completed the paperwork. A curious three year old from a different family cautiously approached the dainty white pup. Her childish exuberance emerged quickly, and her confidence around the furry creature grew. The toddler metamorphosed into an innocent puppy's worst nightmare. As both families watched silently, I observed the poor pup being chased, squeezed and fallen upon.

All dogs deserve to be handled with respect, and adults must monitor and prevent children from pulling, poking, screaming at, squeezing, grabbing, and otherwise tormenting dogs. Youngsters and dogs rarely get along without plenty of supervision and teaching. Unless both child and dog are monitored and schooled, someone is likely to get hurt. Don't ever put your dog, good-natured or not, where he may have to learn to defend himself. A little abuse is never okay.

Give him proper outlets for his energy.

Two veterinary technicians asked how I address chewing problems and went on to explain that their three seven-month-old Rottweiler littermates systematically destroyed some Nylabones. They did not destroy Gumabones or smaller Nylabones, but demolished the large knucklebones. They also mutilated furnishings with beaver-like efficiency.

Rough play will definitely turn your dog into a fighter.

Although the owners were not unduly upset, they probably would have liked to stop the chewing. The first thing that came to mind was to give the dogs some regular, hard exercise. Formal training will stimulate their minds, give them a job to do and reduce the cagey, anxious feeling adolescent dogs experience. Until their energy level and curiosity are properly channeled (for six months perhaps), these dogs need consistent schooling, exercise and supervision.

Agree on rules.

When an owner-trainer, involved in our problem-solving program, is not seeing marked improvement, we assume that our previous recommendations were used unsuccessfully, and we happily offer additional suggestions. But when problems persist, we must ask probing questions and, unfortunately, may uncover underlying tension, abuse or neglect. When household members are fighting among themselves, or sabotaging or disrupting training, human problems must be solved before dog training can begin. In addition to exercise, grooming, proper nutrition and training, dogs need a relatively peaceful household where members agree on rules.

The kids want the dog to jump, beg, bark and run. Dad invites Fido to cuddle on the sofa, but everyone else yells at the dog to get off the furniture. Mom lets the dog pull, and no one else wants to walk a dog who strains at the end of its leash.

Talk to your family and compromise. The family member insistent on keeping the dog in the garage may actually welcome a well-mannered dog into the house. Ask if a dog trained to stay, not to sit on furniture and to chew only on his toys would be an acceptable house dog. If the kids encourage rough play, strike a deal to take the kids and the dog to a favorite park a couple of times a week, and enroll them in a local agility class that teaches obstacles and direction so they can interact with the dog in constructive, interesting and fun ways.

In an ideal world, everyone would expect the same behavior from a dog and treat it accordingly. But, realistically, no two people will treat a dog the same. Because dogs are pack animals, they are accustomed to treating members of their pack with varying degrees of respect. Therefore, the pushover in your household won't necessarily cancel the other members' authority or confuse your dog. He may simply learn a different code of behavior in their presence.

Foxy, a boarding client and extremely noisy traveler, was a good example of a dog's adaptive behavior. She understood and accepted that no barking was tolerated in my car, but every time her owners dropped her off or picked her up, Foxy's announcements could be heard for several blocks. Foxy's selective behavior satisfied her owners, who didn't mind the racket, and me, who insisted on a silent partner.

CHAPTER 5

What's the REAL Problem?

Suppose you come home from work and find your kitchen flooded, again! It's flooded almost every night. Although constantly mopping up the mess annoys you, you never look for the source of the leak. Once in a while you come home to a dry floor, so you continue complaining and cleaning, believing it will eventually stop for good.

GET ANALYTICAL

Now, suppose the wetness is really a puddle left by your dog. You may do one of several things, including cleaning up, getting angry, punishing or confining. Teaching proper toilet habits may not solve the problem. If you have tried unsuccessfully to correct a problem, you may be using the wrong approach. Consider all the reasons behind the problem—body, soul and mind.

Physical Problems

Is the dog properly groomed, sufficiently exercised, nutritiously fed? Is it free of parasites and ailments?

Discomfort because of a matted coat, long nails or excess weight, can trigger or aggravate countless behavioral problems. For instance, the most comprehensive training program can't cure house-soiling problems if the dog has parasites, infections or an improper diet.

Disobedience is learned every time commands are not enforced.

Attending to your dog's good health alone rarely results in perfect behavior. Good behavior must be taught, but to firmly ensure your message is being received, the dog must have a healthy body.

Inattention

Is your dog blocking out your message? Some dogs have a learning barrier—arrogance, distractibility, lack of confidence. Until you establish a new attitude (soul), no amount of training can solve behavioral problems.

If barking and jumping only occur when guests are present, the real problem is actually overexcitability. Use sneakaways to teach the dog to maintain emotional control in those situations, and good manners will come naturally.

Dog training magic—the "sneakaway" is the foundation of Training in No Time, *allowing for easy teaching and effective problem solving by first focusing your dog's undivided attention on you even around the strongest distractions.*

SNEAKAWAY FROM PROBLEMS

Until a dog-training pill is available, the sneakaway is the closest thing to a cure-all. Every problem behavior from house soiling to chewing, every overly emotional reaction from submissive urination to separation anxiety and every antisocial response from aggression to fear can be pruned with hit-or-miss concoctions, but sneakaways will erode them at their root.

Sneakaways teach control and attention despite distractions. Even without addressing specific behaviors, the lessons learned through sneakaways begin a magical transformation and increase every dog's trainability and absorption of information. If you want to reduce your workload, preface all training and problem solving with the sneakaway. Consider the sneakaway as your magic potion and the long line a magic wand!

Think of the sneakaway as playing "hard to get." Hold just the handle of a 15-foot line, let all the slack drag and determinedly walk away any time your dog walks more than five feet from you or acts unfocused. Dogs are attracted to the movement of a handler with an agenda. Scram every time he mentally or physically parts company with you.

Get a Grip on It—Holding the Leash and Line

Place your thumb through the loop of the line or the leash, and grip the handle by covering it with your four fingers. With this grip the handle can never accidentally slip out of your hand, and no matter how large, strong and out of control your dog is, your fingers, hand or wrist will never be injured. Also, if you do need to release the handle, you can do so easily by opening your hand.

The line must be slack when you begin moving away, to allow the dog to be prompt in checking back with you and to follow along to avoid the jerk. But if your dog doesn't follow, the slack line will abruptly tighten, snapping him in your direction with a jerk. Your unpredictable nature gives him reason to be attentive. His interest in you will be rewarded with a perpetually slack line.

The sneakaway is also an effective way to leash-break dogs over four months of age who are unresponsive to coaxing. If you acquire a new dog or you or a family member is having difficulty bonding with a skittish or aloof dog, sneakaways will revive the dog's confidence and enhance his character.

A properly trained dog never shows blatant disregard for the handler when attracted elsewhere. It is bad manners, as is lingering on the telephone while an invited guest is ignored. Additionally, it is dangerous. Pulling, weaving or circling puts the handler at risk of being taken off balance or tripped. The dog may be stepped on or may encroach on an unfriendly dog's territory. Most important, pulling allows a dog to be literally and figuratively ahead of his handler, creating a learning barrier.

Teaching a dog to be aware amidst distractions breaks down the barricade to learning. After two days or when he walks close and keeps his legs tangle-free, train him near intriguing situations that would bring out his worst tendencies and characteristics—jumping, barking, pulling, overexcitability, aggression. Run away immediately when he looks away or contemplates moving toward the distraction. Stop dead when the line goes slack. If your dog stops with you, momentarily stand still before sauntering about. If the dog doesn't stop or remain focused, run in the opposite direction again.

> TROUBLE-SHOOTING TIP   If your dog tries to bite the line or habitually tangles his legs or refuses to move, attach the line to his collar during play periods and as he meanders about the house. Supervise so you correct biting with a spray of Bitter Apple (a chewing deterrent) in the mouth and on the line or a cuff under the muzzle. Resume sneakaways when your dog is no longer preoccupied with mouthing the line or maneuvering his legs over it.

Frustrated trainers often resort to crating while regaining their composure and ability to reevaluate the situation. If you prefer to immediately address your differences, try five minutes of sneakaways in an open area. In moments you'll once again be the master of a calm, happy and focused pal. No violence, no side effects, and it's environmentally safe. No kidding!

MISUNDERSTANDING YOUR DOG'S BODY LANGUAGE

Do you assume your pet knows right from wrong because he acts guilty, meek, evasive, giddy or defensive following inappropriate behavior? Since guilt isn't a canine emotion, what you're actually seeing are his uneasiness and confusion rather than acknowledgment that he knows exactly what is wrong or that he has the power to prevent you from being upset by future incidences of misbehavior.

PARDON ME?
What Do You Mean?
I'm trying to listen to you!

My friend's husband had difficulty communicating. He assumed his wife was intentionally angering him or was just plain thoughtless. Instead of expressing how nice it would be if the cap was replaced on the toothpaste between uses or the towels were folded in thirds instead of quarters, he offered the silent treatment. Since he'd explained his idea of proper household protocol once or twice, in his mind, the transgression was so obvious he assumed she'd think about it and figure it out.

Soon my friend simply walked into the house and could "feel" she once again committed an unknown indiscretion. She felt frustrated, stupid and angry all at once. Soon she was constantly uncomfortable, knowing so many things might displease her spouse, but unable to read his mind and satisfy him. He grew ever more angry about her flagrant negligence. After all, he felt his expectations were fair, his message clear. My friend remedied the situation, but your dog unfortunately can't seek counseling or threaten divorce if he is unhappy about your method of communication.

Training Isn't What We Teach, It's What He Learns

If your timing is off, message unclear or inconsistent or you are expecting the dog to learn faster than his abilities, you are bound to be disappointed.

After-the-fact corrections are seldom effective. In the rare cases they do work, one application does the trick. Therefore, don't abuse your dog physically or verbally every night when you discover he destroyed the house while you were at work. Unless of course you want to have a dog who, in addition to being destructive, is fearful and frustrated.

If your dog raids the laundry basket and then seeks you out to show off what he found, right from wrong is the furthest thing from his mind. Getting your attention is his intent. The time to correct is as he's thinking about snooping. Dogs live for the moment. Corrections must occur before he has captured his prize; otherwise, he'll learn to steal something else, take it to another area and destroy it in a different way.

What's Wrong? Simply Nothing's Right

At the sixth and last lesson of puppy class, Jack was exasperated. His primary reason for attending class was to control his eight-week-old Golden Retriever's continual mouthing. Jack displayed his tooth-scratched hands and lamented that no techniques had been successful in curbing Honey's painful and irritating tendency. Though I suggested he give commands to redirect that energy rather than attempt to forcefully stop the biting, I knew my words would make no difference.

You see, from the first day of class the students were encouraged to use specific techniques to keep this group of unusually noisy pups quiet during the weekly half-hour-long class. Yet Jack made a less than half-hearted attempt to control Honey's incessant yapping. By failing to curb Honey's bratty, persistent vocal outbursts, Jack deprived the class of clearly hearing the discussion and demonstrated his inability to communicate with Honey.

Over the weeks, I recommended that Jack keep Honey leashed and first take full control of Honey's minor misbehaviors like excessive barking. Problems will evaporate with sufficient exercise and sneakaway sessions and by addressing specific minor, followed by major, problems sequentially: first on leash, then at a distance, next off leash and finally when you're absent.

This comprehensive program requires dedication, which isn't easy, but the formula is simple and surefire. With this system, Jack can take the sting out of any killer bee, including Honey!

Temper Tantrums

Typically, just as all appears to be going well and sometimes when it seems things can't get worse, a puppy temper tantrum will strike. Biting, flailing, rearing up, screaming or playing dead may unnerve you to the point of giving up and giving in, believing you may be hurting the poor pup or making an unfair request. Undoubtedly the manipulative pup will snicker as you back off.

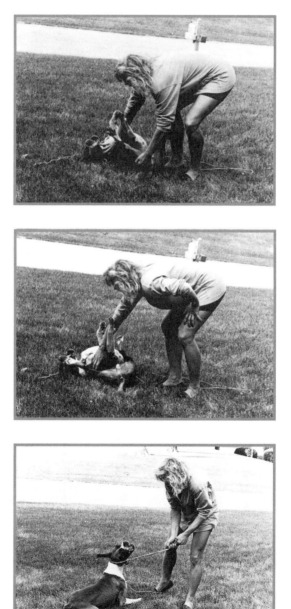

If you are unable to safely grasp the collar of a dog in the throes of a temper tantrum, use the leash to enforce the Come command followed by the Sit command.

Since clever pups routinely use tantrums as a ploy to get their way, keep your cool and diligently pursue your objective. If he's off leash, ignore him. When you can get a leash on him, keep it attached to him in preparation for the next episode. Now, when the resistance antics start in reaction to restraint, correction or commands, say nothing as you tighten the lead, and make him assume a sit or down position. Hold him in position without saying a word until he calms down, then praise him lavishly. If you are truly fearful of getting bitten, contact a trainer experienced in handling aggression to show you exactly what type of correction will be effective with your pup, when to give it and exactly how much force to use so the problem doesn't get worse.

Off-Leash Control

Most owner-trainers are frustrated by disobedience off leash because they see their dogs as perfectly behaved on leash, but off-leash control is actually easy if you're attuned to every misbehavior on leash. Not surprisingly though, it is easy to overlook opportunities to train when your dog is leashed. It seems unnecessary when you can solve problems by restraining. Always think of ways to use your leash like a communication tool.

Try an experiment. Think of the worst temptation for your dog— guests, children, other dogs. Find those distractions, and without ever touching or holding the leash, see how your dog responds to nonthreatening commands. Avoid touching the leash. Instead, walk to his collar to make an "off-leash-type correction" by grabbing his collar. Just think of how you would enforce commands if he were actually off leash.

But wait—why would you have to enforce? You claimed your dog was perfect on leash. No matter how well trained, no dog is ever perfect. Therefore, before giving commands off leash, practice around distractions with the leash dragging until, in the rare event he disobeys, the dog doesn't dodge you as you reach for his collar to correct.

Wonderful Leash-Walking Manners

You can learn about people by studying their walk. Character is revealed by their pace, stride and posture. Inner strength, overwhelming stress or lack of confidence are reflected in every step.

Next time you see a dog walking on leash, look for clues about the dog-owner relationship. Is the dog moving at his own pace, oblivious to the owner's speed, direction or desires? Does he bark at passersby or sniff, pull, lag and weave? Is he content to stay by the owner if there is nothing better to do, but when he sees a fun time, does he have his own agenda? Like a spoiled child who pouts, screams, pounds his feet and cries, this demanding dog is unlikely to take direction when it is most needed. Imagine this dog unleashed as he sees children playing in the distance. It is hoped no cars are coming as he runs to join the party, unconcerned with his owner who trails, yelling commands.

Then there is the tough, stilted, straining strider who enjoys towing his obedient posse. He is confident and proud of his status and seriously protects the earned position. Be prepared for resistance, defensiveness and possibly retaliation if you ask the "terminator" to do anything that conflicts with his plans. He isn't afraid of confrontation.

It is remarkable that dogs, like people, can change their destiny, character and mood by first changing their walk. People can regain childlike optimism by skipping and laughing for a half hour. Insist that your dog be aware and considerate every time you are holding a lead to which he's attached. He should feel under your control even when he isn't under command. Regardless of distractions, he should prefer to be near you because he feels a sense of belonging. **No one rule will do more to keep your dog in check than enforcing no pulling on daily walks.**

After one week of long-line sneakaways, leash your dog and teach him to walk calmly at your left side. Allow the leash to drape across the front of your thighs as you hold it in your right hand, with your thumb through the loop and your four fingers gripping the slack. Anchor your leash-holding right hand to your right hip. Now, if the dog attempts to walk behind you, he'll be pulled into position as your left thigh hits the leash with your every step.

Prevent pulling by pivoting right 180 degrees as you drop the slack and run. The full slack of a six-foot leash allows the dog to experience a sharp jerk that encourages a closer position in the future.

Don't give any commands; otherwise you'll forever have to remind him, and he'll never learn to be under control unless he is under command. Leadership and respect are in order every time you attach a leash. In a balanced human-canine relationship a dog walks beside his owner and doesn't bolt when the feeling strikes. He sticks close because he wants to know "what are we doing together?" He isn't commanded to do it; he is simply under control, level-headed and with his emotions in check.

Preventative Dog Training

You can teach a dog many things, but because you are reading *Training in No Time*, you're probably looking for the most practical and effortless training possible. I was at a computer seminar explaining the benefits of computerization for retailers. The leader explained the benefits and simplification of computerization. An audience member wanted to cross-reference the prices of 12 different suppliers, allowing him to pick the lowest cost at a glance. He quickly realized that the labor required to log in the information wouldn't be worth the convenience; so it is with dog training. You can teach your dog not to dig in the backyard when you are at work, but you'd have to spy on him hour after hour, day after day for weeks or months to break the habit. Then, if he digs when you've let your guard down, you must repeat the process. Consider the advantage of kenneling your companion in a dig-proof enclosure during working hours.

It is hoped that you have better things to do besides train your dog, so before correcting a problem, ask yourself if it is easier to prevent or avoid. Avoiding these no-no's will prevent many common misbehaviors.

1. Too-rough play encourages biting and overexcitability.
2. Excited arrivals encourage separation anxiety, submissive urination and pandemonium when guests arrive.
3. Feeding anything besides dog food or feeding out of hand or anywhere near a traffic pattern will encourage begging, jumping, possessiveness, aggression and picky appetite.
4. Leaving garbage receptacles uncovered, not immediately removing tasty garbage and wrappers from the house, leaving cabinets or dishwashers open and having laundry, cat litter boxes or personal items accessible encourages stealing and scavenging in garbage cans, on counters and in closets.
5. Unsupervised time outdoors encourages overbarking, and, if the dog is not enclosed in a concrete run, digging, destruction and potential injury to humans or other animals entering the territory.
6. Giving the dog soft toys, personal items and raglike toys to chew on encourages inappropriate chewing. Stuffed toys, shoes and upholstered-type items are some things you never want your dog to acquire a taste for. If your veterinarian recommends them, supply him with Nylabones, sterilized bones, rawhides and cowhooves as an outlet for his hard-chewing needs.

The ultimate red flag for misbehavior of trained dogs is upsetting their routines. A streak of unusually hot, cold or wet weather that alters your activity level; tension in the household because of strained human relationships; a change in members or a move is stressful, so don't expect normal behavior under abnormal circumstances.

Problem-Solving System

Your dog is exercised, groomed and well nourished. He respects you because of sneakaways, but he still has naughty habits that you can't solve by environmental changes. Here are the six steps to righting all those wrongs.

Practice Being Right

Let's assume the problem is stealing from the garbage can, and the chain of events looks like this: At least once a week for the last weeks, months or years Fido has sampled everything from tissue to cheese wrappers from the waste cans. Monday morning, on discovering another raid, you vow to catch him next time and show him the error of his ways. Sure enough, Tuesday you catch him with his snout in the trash can and correct him. Although he didn't like the correction, he is likely to repeat the deed soon, because the satisfaction of the previous day's successful raid is equally fresh, tempting him to risk the consequences yet again.

Let the memories of misbehavior fade. Only employ the corrections after two weeks of abstinence from garbage picking, lunging or whatever bugs you.

Eliminate the Window of Opportunity

To ensure your dog abstains from misbehaving before and during reconditioning, find a place where your dog can do no wrong when you're unable to supervise him. Crating or confining in a dig-proof, chew-proof area works best. Always practice teaching your dog to enter the enclosure on command before closing him in.

Simply lead him to the opening and point inside as you tell him to enter. Pull him in by the collar, praise, invite him out. Repeat five times in a row, five times a day until he walks in on command.

When you are at home, ensure constant supervision by umbilical cording. Have you ever run to the bathroom and found your dog did too? Since it only takes a second to make a mistake, keep your dog by your side. Tying him to your belt with a short leash enables you to monitor him and prevent him from jumping, barking, chewing or soiling.

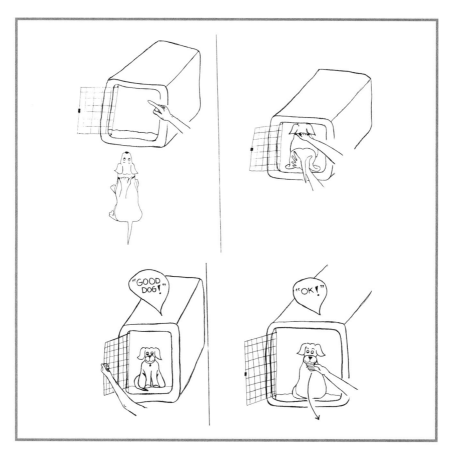

Crate Training

Successful crate training is achieved through these simple, yet effective steps.

To get the dog to enter the crate:

1. Hold the dog by its collar.

2. Point to the inside of the crate with your free hand and tell him to enter.

3. Help the dog into the crate by keeping one hand on its collar, and with the other, apply gentle pressure from behind.

To keep the dog in the crate (with the door open):

4. Enforce the "Wait" command.

5. With one hand on the open crate door, praise the dog, but be prepared to give him a corrective nose tap if he tries to exit on his own.

To remove the dog (on command) from the crate:

6. Invite the dog to leave the crate by touching the dog's chin with your hand while saying, "Okay!"

7. Move your hand toward your own body, withdrawing it from the crate.

Repeat all steps five times in a row, several times each day until the actions have been learned. Some people prefer to use a command word when training a dog to enter a crate so that the dog will eventually enter the crate simply upon hearing the word.

Our dogs are most likely to get into some kind of mischief when we are otherwise preoccupied, and they are left to their own devices.

Consistency

Haphazard enforcement is responsible for most problem-solving failures. If he's only corrected at your convenience, he is actually being taught to misbehave at certain times. Naturally, problem-solving techniques are only effective if they are used EACH time the misbehavior occurs.

Distract or Deter

Stopping undesirable behavior can be done in three ways—change environment, change focus or correct. If your dog barks during meals: You could change the environment by tying him outside or putting him in another room or eating away from home; or you could change his focus by giving him a fascinating toy or tasty treat or by telling him to Down and Stay; or you could stop him from barking with a jerk of the

Feeding your dog in an inappropriate framework will give rise to bad habits such as garbage raiding, jumping on people and begging at the dinner table.

leash, an application of Bitter Apple, a cuff under the jaw, a scruff shake, a toss of a shaker can or a shot of water from a spray bottle. Use whatever approach that is just repulsive enough to deter him.

Decide which of the three approaches works best for the problem at hand and use it.

Setup (only necessary if problem solving involves correction rather than environmental or focus change)

Find a way to make him misbehave when you're ready to correct. Initially, it might not be necessary because he is always naughty. After a few corrections he should be more selective about misbehaviors. He still won't actually know what is expected, unless you put him to the test. Setups are also a good way to confirm what he knows. Think entrapment and irresistible temptation.

Bridget had a very well-mannered German Shepherd Dog who chewed her partially raveled carpeting one day while she was at work. Bridget swore he'd never touch it when she was home, so I suggested she rub some liver sausage on a remnant of the same carpeting. By placing it over the chewed spot, Fritz was likely to show interest in the area when she was home and able to correct. It worked!

Gradual Trust

If you've chosen to change the environment or change focus, you may need to do that for the rest of your dog's life. If you're correcting, repeat realistic setups until your dog refuses them time after time over a period of weeks or months before allowing short periods of unsupervised freedom. Gradually extend the time, then see how he does for a short period when you leave the house.

Timing Is Everything Quiz

Poorly timed, poorly administered, inconsistent corrections occasionally produce desirable results. Test your ability to think like a dog.

Question 1

Dudley messes on the porch instead of on the lawn. After stepping in it, his owner, Matt, hops on one foot over to Dudley, drags him to the mess, scolds him, then tosses him on the grass. Dudley learns to:

A. Not mess in the yard, on the porch or on the grass. Now, if Matt wants to make sure Dudley doesn't soil in the house, he has to walk him.

B. Eat his mess, so there is no evidence he soiled the porch.

C. Next time Matt discovers a mess on the stoop, Dudley:

    1. Plays keep away from his maniac owner.

    2. Runs to look at his mess, then leaps on the grass.

All the above are possible.

Matt can solve this problem by teaching Dudley to go potty on command and by using a chant like "potty hurry up" every time the dog eliminates. Then he'd issue the chant from the back door, poised and ready to interrupt Dudley's concentration if he tried to mess on the porch. For months, Matt would make sure he always supervised Dudley's activity in the backyard, waiting for a chance to correct. Dudley would be considered trained with freedom earned only after weeks of using the area without a verbal or visual reminder.

Question 2

Pam is getting ready for work and can find only one sock. After searching for another pair and changing her entire outfit to match, Pam is now behind schedule. She rushes downstairs intent on quickly crating Spunky, her Toy Fox Terrier, so she can arrive at the office on time.

Around a corner, Spunky stands, tail wagging slowly, ready to grab the missing sock positioned at her feet. Pam threatens to beat Spunky with the *Wall Street Journal*, and that sends her running gleefully just out of Pam's reach. After being ignored all morning, Spunky delights in suddenly having Pam's undivided attention.

Rodney, Pam's spouse and the alpha member of the household, comes to the rescue by booming, "No!" Spunky flees under the table with her head low and tail tucked. She huddles in the corner, too terrified to come out on her own. Pam is unable to grasp the collar and pull her out as Spunky rolls on her back, kicking her paws and snapping at Pam's hand. Spunky has learned to:

A. Fear bite.

B. Chew on different things in a different way in a different area (shred slippers under the bed).

C. Run away when called.

D. Get into mischief as a way to demand attention.

All the above are possible.

Tracing the progression of the misbehavior, Pam would find it began when Spunky nosed open the closet door and reached into the sock bin. Therefore, Pam must be more cautious about keeping taboo items out of reach and more careful to correct Spunky as she investigates the sock bin. Tracing misbehavior applies to correcting jumping up on

counters or people, stealing of trash, unrolling of the toilet tissue or destroying of household items or landscape.

Question 3

Marge is walking Bandit on leash and he lunges. Marge digs her heels into the ground and holds onto the leash for dear life with both hands. Oblivious to the restraint and Marge's reassuring voice repeating, "No, no, no, it's okay!" Bandit drags his mistress over to attack a passing dog. Bandit has just learned:

A. Marge praises him when he lunges.

B. His lunging scares other dogs away.

C. He owns the sidewalk.

All the above are possible.

Marge should interrupt the dog's focus on the target of his aggression with surprise, pain or by assigning a duty. Surprise could come in the form of a spray of water, the tap of a ring of keys on the forehead or a hit of the shaker can. Pain might be a jerk of the collar. The duty would be obedience to a sit, down or heel command. To break an aggressive dog's concentration, intervene when you think he begins stiffening, raising hackles, piercing eye contact. Correcting full-fledged aggression is almost impossible, unless Marge is the strongest woman in the world, capable of halting a speeding locomotive in a split second. Control the aggression before velocity has a chance to build.

Question 4

Happy is barking in the backyard. Mark yells, "Shush!" She continues barking. The neighbors complain about the noise. Mark rushes out to quiet her. Happy stops barking when she sees Mark, knowing he's likely to hit her, torpedo objects at her or spray her. As soon as Mark is out of sight, Happy resumes barking. Mark finally brings her in the house. Mark has just taught Happy to:

A. Ignore commands.

B. Shy away from him.

C. Bark until he lets her in.

All the above are possible.

Barking is a great attention-getting ploy. Make sure the dog doesn't receive positive attention for useless barking. Mark should teach the "Quiet" command up close, then when Happy is tied outside, attach a second leash to her collar that is long enough for him to hold as he walks out of sight. Now, if Happy ignores the quiet command, Mark can instantly correct with a jerk, instead of rewarding the noise with his presence and attention.

CHAPTER 6

Social Studies

Canine "Social Studies" should include vocabulary lessons and preparation for meetings and common interactions. Teach commands and proper behavior around food and guests, in the car, in all public places and when your dog is alone, to ensure that his well-rounded education will merit your trust.

PART 1—VOCABULARY

Command-Training System

Any command is easy to teach when you follow this system. Whether using whistles, hand signals or verbal commands, the general rules of teaching your dog to obey are always the same.

Define the Intent

Even the most basic command can mean different things. To the obedience trial competition dog, Sit means to plop its bottom on the ground—quickly, squarely and attentively, waiting for the next direction as its feet remain positioned just so. When you issue a command, what exact position, speed and duration do you expect? If you don't know, then postpone training until you figure it out. Otherwise, your lack of direction will confuse and frustrate your dog.

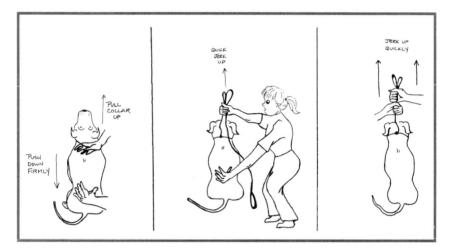

The Sit and the Sit-Stay

Step 1: Teach with Pull Up and Push Down.

a. Place hand on dog's loin.

b. Hold collar with opposite hand.

c. Say dog's name and command "Sit" while pulling straight up on collar as rear is pushed down.

Step 2: Enforce with Jerk Up and Push Down.

a. Say dog's name and command "Sit" once.

b. Wait a moment.

c. If necessary, correct with a quick upward jerk and light push down.

Step 3: Correct with a two-handed Jerk.

a. Command "Sit."

b. Wait a moment.

c. Place one hand above the other, six inches from snap, and quickly jerk straight up.

Define the Cue

You need two cues, one to begin the action and one to end it. One-word verbal commands, preceded by the dog's name, work best. Commands can be ended by issuing another command (a Down command would supersede the Sit, for instance) or by releasing the dog from duty with a word like "Okay" or a phrase like, "That'll do." A common release word can be used to end any request.

TROUBLE-SHOOTING TIP: CHIN-TOUCH OKAY   If "Okay" is your release word of choice, then pair it with a gentle touch under the chin so he doesn't break his commands every time he hears you use "Okay" in conversation. For the first three weeks, step forward along with the "Chin-Touch Okay" to encourage the dog to move off his command when released.

Use Proper Tone and Volume

Issue verbal commands with serious clarity. Don't let an edge of anger, loud-mouthing or scolding take the place of proper training. If you don't get the proper response, then review ground rules and evaluate where the message was lost.

Decide on Reinforcement

Find out what works best by reading, watching tapes, going to class and trying what sounds logical. You may need different reinforcements for the same exercise, depending on whether he's learning, confused or distracted. For instance, when working on "Sit," teach with a push on the loin and upward pull on the collar. Use the same technique if he is confused, but jerk up if he is too distracted to respond to a familiar command.

While Teaching, Pair Reinforcement with Command

Dogs have different aptitudes for different tasks. While teaching any dog, eagerly, happily and consistently, always implement the proper

response along with the command, so that the individual dog can learn as quickly as possible. Never expect one dog to learn as fast as another.

Show Appreciation with Praise

Enthusiastically speak sweet words of praise. Return a subtle smile, blink and nod as your dog gazes up at you. Know what your dog looks like when he is happiest and learn how to elicit that reaction.

Test Your Dog's Understanding

Because he did it right, don't assume he knows that; it could have happened by accident or by default. A trained dog does it right regardless of the circumstances, so test him under various difficult conditions.

Never Take Obedience for Granted

Even the best student's knowledge will fade over time. Be a good teacher and anticipate the need to give your dog occasional reminders.

Sit—The Easiest Command, So Make the Demand

Hold your dog's collar with one hand, and place the other hand on his loin (across his back in his waistline). Now, as you command "Sit," pull up on his collar and place his rear. Praise and never repeat your command or allow your dog to move before releasing. Remember, dogs live for the moment, and you need to praise the action of sitting. If you say "Sit," "Okay," "Good!" you've just praised him for moving, but he needs praise for doing the unnatural act—sitting.

Once he knows the command but refuses to act because of laziness or distractibility, correct simultaneously with a quick upward leash jerk and a very light-handed, downward push on his rear. After a few weeks of using the jerk and push correction, simply jerk upward to correct. Otherwise, because dogs love to be touched, you may find he thinks the jerk and push is a reward for not sitting.

The Three Quickest Ways to Get Respect

Never Repeat, Never Wait for Respect and Never Tolerate Pulling

Dogs have fantastic hearing for important noises. Just try quietly opening a candy wrapper. Most dogs will hear it from the farthest corner of the house. They also have great memories for the smell of the veterinarian's office, the route to the park and what time family members come home. Whether teaching or enforcing commands, the louder you speak and the more you repeat commands, the less important they become. Ultimately, you'll find that your dog is obeying less reliably and that you're giving louder commands and repeating yourself more

often to get the desired response. You'd never learn a foreign language if the teacher yelled unfamiliar words over and over. Only the coupling of the action with the words will make the meaning clear.

While it may seem logical to wait for your dog's attention before giving a command, doing so only reinforces lack of urgency and respect. If your dog is really distracted, recapture attention by sneaking away, but if he's simply daydreaming, then quickly issue the command with authority and praise. He'll never be bored or lackadaisical if you treat requests with urgency and show appreciation for his compliance, whether he had a choice or you made it happen.

Again, always enforce the no-pulling rule with sneakaways. Whether walking to the car, talking with a friend or at the vet's office, maintain control.

Stay Frozen

Not only is the Stay one of the most useful commands for calming down a dog, for keeping him out of trouble and for examining and grooming, but it is also the easiest command to teach reliably, if you've done the proper groundwork. Your dog should respond reliably in all situations to Sit and Down commands and stay until released as you and anyone else praise lavishly.

Sit him, position the collar high around his neck and keep upward tension on the leash. Command "Stay," walk one step away and act busy. Since the Stay will be most valuable when you are preoccupied, busy yourself by examining or picking things up, tying your shoe or talking to someone. Watch your dog from the corner of your eye so you can silently reposition him into the Sit as he begins raising his rear. Every few seconds, briefly step back to his side to praise, then continue busying yourself. Release with an "Okay" and the chin touch after about a minute.

Before walking two steps away, gradually increase the time and temptation by practicing in different surroundings. If you leash your dog to walk him, practice the Stay daily as you put your jacket on, say "hello" to a neighborhood dog, retrieve the mail or open the door.

Stay Frozen

The "Stay Frozen" command keeps your dog under control when you are together and your attention is focused elsewhere, making this command especially useful while you and your dog are in public.

1. Make the dog sit.

2. Position yourself one step away.

3. Keep tension on the lead.

4. Act busy but remain aware of the dog's intentions.

5. If the dog moves or rises, quickly correct him by placing him back in the original Sit position.

Distance Stay

After a week or two, your dog should be reliable enough to move farther away, but don't drop that leash unless you'd bet all your past training successes that, no matter what the temptation, Fido would NEVER move. Eliminate the risk of letting your dog know that you have no control by tying his long line to something stationary. Then maneuver him so he sits facing away from where he's tied. When the line is attached to his collar it should be slack so he feels unrestrained. Now your hands are free, and you can move farther away and act busy.

If he moves, the line will prevent his escape, and the leash will allow you to silently and quickly move him back to the spot where you left him. Jerk him up to sit him before returning to your busy work.

Distance Stay

1. *Tie a line to a stationary object.*
2. *Sit the dog facing away from the stationary object.*
3. *Snap line onto collar.*
4. *Walk away from the dog.*
5. *Act busy.*
6. *If the dog moves from the Sit-Stay, quickly reposition him.*
7. *Return to your previous activity.*

Out of Sight Stay

Develop greater respect by demonstrating that commands are enforceable even when your dog can't see you. This also is necessary for

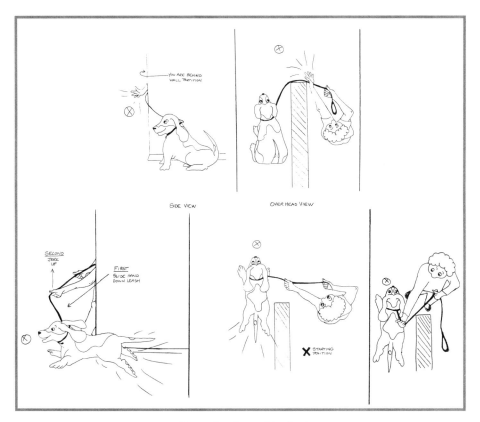

Teaching the Out of Sight Stay

1. *Sit the dog alongside a wall partition.*
2. *Walk around the partition, holding the lead taut.*
3. *Toss out toys to create a distraction.*
4. *If dog moves, quickly step toward him, slide your hand down the lead and jerk up.*
5. *Return to your out of sight position.*
6. *Try the exercise again.*

correcting bad manners that only occur when you're preoccupied or away and for controlling separation anxiety. To practice out of sight Stays, position your dog next to the corner of a building so you can hold the leash as you walk around the corner. Without letting him know your location, throw toys, food and intriguing things past him. Since he can't see you and he has no idea how far away you are, the temptation to move is irresistible. Prepare to correct movement by sliding your hand down the leash to his collar and then jerking up. Leave as quickly as you appeared.

Practical Uses

With daily enforcement of the Stay, in about four weeks your dog should reliably obey as you do simple tasks like unloading groceries, folding laundry and grooming.

Wait Around

When you want to leave your dog in the car as you step into the grocery store or keep your dog out of an off-limits area like your white-carpeted living room, what command should be given? "Stay" will prevent him from leaving the car or entering the off-limits area, but didn't you just show your dog that "Stay" means to freeze in position? Since it isn't necessary that your dog remain frozen while you shop or relax in the formal room, teach another command that instructs your dog to stay in an area.

To understand the difference between "Stay" and "Wait," visualize the behavior expected of a child who is instructed to *stay* sitting in his high chair versus one who is asked to *wait* in his room. Begin by teaching your dog to remain in the house by casually opening an exterior door a few inches. Issue the Wait command just before opening the door, regardless of whether the dog is across the room or in front of the door. This designates the area beyond the doorway off limits, so the trained dog usually won't bother to approach, making it easy for people to come and go.

To enforce the "Wait" command, open the door only about as wide as the dog's shoulders. If he ignores your command and tries to pass through the door, close it just enough to stop his forward progress.

Accepting deliveries is not stressful if you have control with the Wait command before you actually take your package.

Applying restraint will amplify problem behavior.

If you fail to get control of your dog while your guests are at the door, then trouble is guaranteed when they enter your home.

A dog that is reliable at the door makes the comings and goings of people at your home eminently more pleasant for all concerned.

Leave the door open with your hand on the door handle, ready to stop attempted departures with an abrupt and silent bump of the door. Since he can't learn not to go through an opening that doesn't exist, be sure never to shut the door while correcting. Rather, use the door to tap the dog's snout so the opening is inviting except during the momentary correction. Make it appear that the door is snapping at his nose every time he peers out. The procedure is the same whether the door opens in or out. Leash your dog and practice alone at lightweight doors until you feel confident about the timing and strength necessary to deter your dog.

Practice at familiar and unfamiliar doors as a helper tries to coerce your dog to leave. As your guest remains on the other side of the door, engage in lively conversation to teach your dog that Wait is enforced even when you are preoccupied. Then apply the technique at heavy or sliding doors, off leash and when people are actually coming or going.

Cross Over

After saying "Wait" and opening the door, hesitate before you or your guests pass through the door. You may need to give a reminding correction to convince him to back off so you can easily pass through. Should he try to slip out as you're in the doorway, use your knee to bump him back.

Out of Sight

Enforce the Wait from behind a door. Begin by commanding "Wait" at a door that opens out, hesitate, cross over the doorway so you are standing behind the door, hand on knob, completely out of sight. Throw distractions and have children run in and out as you watch, ready to tap his snout with the door should his nose appear in the opening. Now, whether or not you are present, he'll respect your command.

Come, Come Now

Each time your dog wants to come, for example, when he hears you preparing his food or getting ready for a walk, call him, run away and praise. While he is following intently, continue praising as you squat

Teaching the Come Command

1. *Call your dog to you.*
2. *Reel him in to you.*
3. *Praise him when he is in the correct position.*

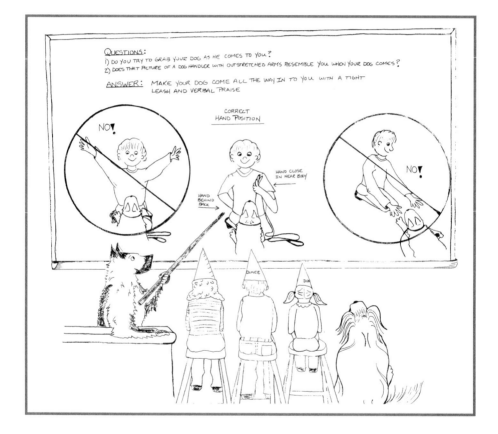

down with hands folded behind your back. Tell him how adorable he is, but don't pet him unless he is nuzzling closely. Even then, beware of grabbing. Scratch him under the chin or on his sides or on his tummy if he is lying down. While he is still reveling in the affection, say "Okay," stand and abruptly walk away. He'll work harder for your affection if it is enthusiastic but short.

In addition, work on "Come" around distractions. With leash attached, take your dog to a distraction-filled area and call, "Buster, Come," when he is preoccupied. Back up to use his chase instinct, reeling the leash in to ensure his response. After a week of practice, stop doing all the work for him by reeling in the leash, and, instead, begin the correction phase. Call, wait a second to see if he responds, then back up and praise. If he ignores your command, jerk the leash toward you as you back up and praise.

Even when he responds reliably, encourage a supercharged recall by exuberantly running away and cheering on his reaction like a thoroughbred entering the homestretch in first place.

Never Use Your Dog

Reward your dog each time you ask him to go in, out, up, down, on or off. Otherwise, you may find your dog gets his entertainment by leading you in a chase around the house when you ask him to come in the house, car or tub. Although you probably called him for a reason, treat his response to the Come as a separate event. To ensure eager responses, frequently call him to come for no reason other than to praise, and practice telling him to go in and out of the house, car or crate when you aren't going to ride, confine or leave.

Down for the Count

What single command could stop a runaway dog or prevent "Curious George" from entering a dangerous area, calm an excitable dog, allow grooming and medicating procedures like brushing, examining for fleas,

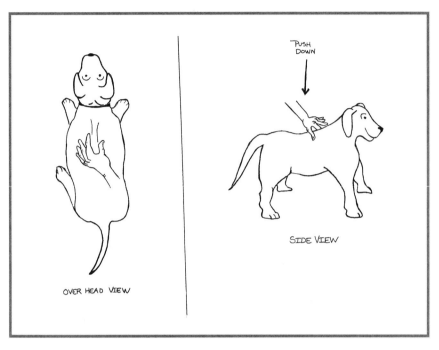

PUSH DOWN

SIDE VIEW

OVER HEAD VIEW

Teaching the Down Command
1. Push down on the dog's back just behind the shoulder blades.
2. Command "Down."

nail cutting and paw examination, and keep a dog away from the table during mealtimes or out of any area where he is unwanted? The Down is the very versatile, useful command that can accomplish these controls and more for your dog.

Some dogs have difficulty learning or are inclined to resist the Down, but this command merits the extra effort it may require. Dominant dogs usually brace, playful and belligerent dogs will mouth, and submissive dogs will love the attention of being placed. Depending on your dog, Down him by rolling, pushing or toppling.

Easy Does It–Style Down

Gentle, submissive, and young dogs can usually be downed by pushing on the back while pulling downward on the collar. First, placing the palm of one hand on the shoulder blades or back of the neck and holding the collar under the dog's chin with the other hand, command "Down" while applying downward pressure on the back and collar. Hold him down as you talk sweetly. Pet him, too, before releasing with the Chin-Touch Okay.

Pressure-Point–Style Down

If your dog braces or needs more incentive to convince him to Down without the aid of your push, find the pressure point along his spine just behind his shoulder blades. Make a U-shape, using thumb and index finger, and place them around the backbone. Pull him down by the collar as you command "Down," and use the two-finger touch behind the shoulder blades to push him downward. Think of using your fingers like a fork to make the dog go "hobbyhorse" into the Down.

From Rigid to Pushover—the Surefire Down

So your dog braces like a marble statue? With a wrestling-type maneuver, gently flip him onto his side. Sit him at your left side and face his profile as you get on one knee. Place your left palm, fingertips pointing skyward, on his right shoulder, and reach under his chest to hold his left front leg with your right hand. Now, simultaneously command "Down" as you pull the far leg toward you while pushing the inner shoulder away to take him off balance.

Never try to Down a dog who protests the Sit or touching of his leg. Teach the dog to accept all manipulation by building respect with sneakaways. Then enforce Sit-Stays as you repeat handling procedures until the dog no longer struggles because he's concentrating on your command.

Variations

Teach your dog to Down regardless of his position by practicing when he's sitting, standing and moving, either at your side or anywhere within arm's reach. Make him Down where he was commanded, or he'll learn to crawl instead of drop. Stop him in his tracks with a horizontal snap of the lead opposite his movement.

After a month of practice, enforce the Down using a diagonal jerk and pressure-point push to ensure a prompt response. When the dog is at your left side, hold the snap of the leash with your right hand, place your left hand in the pressure point and jerk the lead toward the dog's right hind foot while applying the "pressure-point push." That will get him down fast and prevent his mouthing your hand. Also, dogs who love to be petted usually regard the touch alone as a reward for disobedience. The jerk and push allows you to minimize hand-to-dog contact.

Insist he Down instantly on command, whether or not he is looking at you. Avoid using a hand signal. Once you can stand behind him and he responds to a verbal command to Down, teach the distance Down. Randomly Down him five times a day while he's meandering about the house and not expecting a command. Perfect times to command are while reading, folding laundry, doing kitchen duties or other household chores. Begin by dropping him five feet away and by increasing gradually to twenty feet. Demand a prompt drop whether he is running or walking, indoors or out.

Down-Stays

Begin the "Down-Stay" once your dog will Down regardless of his speed or location and will perform an out-of-sight Sit-Stay. Command "Down," then "Stay" and keep the leash slack. Stay close, kneel down, circle and step over your dog and praise him often. Immediately upon seeing daylight under your dog's chest, maneuver him back into position using the "push and jerk." Perfect the Down-Stay from one step away around distractions and when you examine his head, body and feet, before increasing distance and going out of sight.

The Down-Stay is an easy exercise when handlers don't teach disobedience by allowing the command to evaporate. If you remember you are responsible for ending the command with "Chin-Touch Okay," the dog's memory and reliability will never let you down.

JERK LEASH DOWN
TOWARDS DOG'S BACK TOE

OVER HEAD VIEW

The "Jerk Down" Maneuver
(For correcting trained dogs that ignore commands or break Down-Stays)
1. Hold the leash by the snap.
2. Jerk leash down toward the dog's back toe.
3. Resort to Jerk and Push if Jerk alone is ineffective.

Off: aka "Get Your Paws Off and Don't Jump Up"

If you never want your dog to jump, correct silently. Take him off balance with a sharp knee bump to the chest, a jerk of the leash opposite the direction of his jump, or slide your toe sideways under his rear feet. You can also discourage him with a light tap of your open palm on his nostrils.

If you sometimes approve of your dog's jumping on people or furniture, say "Off" as you correct. Even after he knows the Off command, you may have to remind him often with a correction, particularly around guests and children. Therefore, seriously consider the advantages of never allowing jumping up under any circumstances.

Never use the leash simply as a means of restraint when you have the opportunity to communicate good behavior to your dog through the traditional physical link.

Snapping the leash to take the dog off balance is the easiest correction for jumping. It requires no aim, can be done from a distance, and if someone else says "Off" as the dog jumps, it appears that's who is in control regardless of who snaps the leash.

Sliding your toe along the ground under the dog's feet is a great correction for jumping. It is effective for dogs of all sizes whether they are on leash or not and whether you are in front of or behind the dog.

Timing is very important in delivering a "knee bump" correction for the dog with a habit of jumping on people. The correction must be made quickly and before the dog's front paws land on his target.

After several light nose taps, simply raise your palm as if preparing to make the correction and command "Off" to curtail the undesirable behavior.

Quiet, Please

There is nothing wrong with a dog's barking, if you can silence him easily when necessary. Feel free to praise and encourage your dog for appropriate barking, for example, when an intruder is near. But it isn't necessary for a dog's well-being that he be allowed to bark, so if you find all barking disturbing or unacceptable, correct it all.

Teach the Quiet command by leashing your dog and creating a situation likely to elicit barking, perhaps in response to seeing another dog, or during play, around guests or when you're on the telephone. Command "Quiet" when he vocalizes and distract him with a sharp jerk of the leash or a quick squirt of Bitter Apple against his lip as you hold his cheek to ensure accuracy. Praise when he is quiet. After a half-dozen corrections, issue the command and only correct when necessary. If commanding from a distance or when the dog is tied outside, in a kennel or crated, attach a long leash to jerk, or run up to squirt and leave quickly.

TROUBLE-SHOOTING TIP: Never threaten your dog with Bitter Apple or a shaker can. Warning him to behave as you expose your ammunition will only teach respect for the bottle or can. To teach him to respect *you*, wait until he has disobeyed to show how you intend to back it up. Therefore, keep your reinforcements secret by keeping them silent and hidden, before and after use.

Correct barking only when your dog is relatively relaxed. If he is lunging or distracted, get control with sneakaways outdoors or the Wait command in the house. An alternative to correcting noise is to change his focus by giving a command like Sit, Down or Come in rapid-fire sequence for a couple of minutes.

Drop It

Puppies especially like to chew, carry and mouth anything they can—hands, clothing, the leash, gravel, cigarette butts, landscaping timbers,

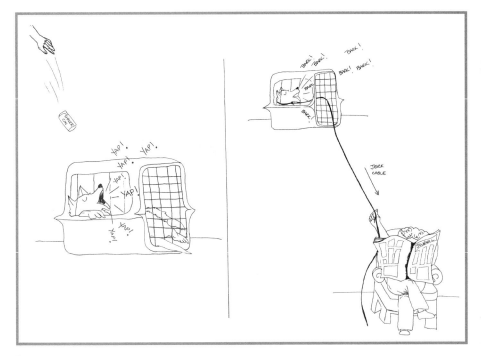

Quiet, Please

You don't have to tolerate an excessively noisy dog. Here are some options for peace and quiet and an enhanced environment for all within earshot!

Option 1. Correct barking by throwing a shaker can at the back of the crate.

Option 2. The cable-jerk method—Place the dog in its crate with a cable attached to the snap on the collar. Close crate door and feed the cable through the grid in the door. Now, if the dog barks in its crate you can pull on the cable to correct the barking.

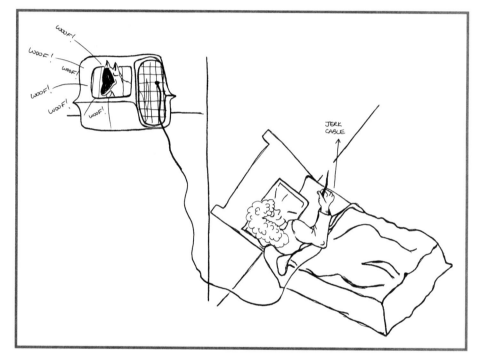

Option 3. The plan of attack here is similar to that of Option 2 but operates with a longer cable if you are in bed, in another room, outside, etc.

tissue. Use one word to mean both "get that out of your mouth" and "don't put that in your mouth." Accompany the "Drop It" command with a sharp jerk of the leash, then quickly offer an acceptable toy with which to play. Tap it on the ground, hide it behind your back and run away with it. Don't relinquish it to your dog until you've played keep away for a few seconds. If the jerk is ineffective, spray your finger with

Teach the "Quiet" command when your dog is next to you. Grasp his cheek to insure accurate aim as you deliver a quick spray of Bitter Apple to enforce the command.

Never use that bottle of Bitter Apple as a threat. Keep it out of sight when it's not being used, and don't look at the dog immediately after making a correction.

Use a jerk of a second lead to correct barking at a distance or when you are out of sight. First, though, teach the Quiet at your side.

Bitter Apple and touch his gum with the sprayed finger as you issue your command. Always praise lavishly and offer an alternative when your dog drops the taboo item.

PART 2—MANNERS AND ETIQUETTE

Getting Ready for Visitors

Dogs are always more likely to misbehave around guests, and owners are more likely to take note of the dog's behavior when guests arrive. The daily practices described in this section will ensure you avoid embarrassment. Behave in the way you'd like your dog to mirror, and his good manners will reflect back at you.

Calm Arrivals and Departures

How do you greet your dog and acknowledge his initial excitement? Do you encourage it? Are you flattered, exasperated or delighted by it, or does it depend on the situation? Eager greetings can be great for your ego, but they foster neurotic behavior. Lay aside the mistaken notion that enthusiastic greetings have any connection to affection, bonding or a healthy relationship. If you are ever frustrated or embarrassed or angered by your dog's physical demonstrations of hyperbole, treat all arrivals and departures as nonevents.

1. If your dog is confined when you come home but doesn't have to be fed, watered or exercised, sometimes ignore him for a few minutes or hours before releasing him.

2. Whether you release him from confinement or walk into the house when your dog has free run, ignore him for 15 minutes. No matter whether you've been in Europe for three weeks or just walked to the post office or have picked him up from the vet, treat every return as if you just stepped out for a moment. Play, fun and enthusiasm are an important part of a well-balanced, bonded relationship, which should never be associated with a person's comings and goings.

Make it a habit to busy yourself doing other things, oblivious to your dog's prancing, barking, jumping or panting. Insist guests and family members do the same. Practice calm arrivals by tying the dog and walking purposely in and out of his tied circumference with your arms folded, avoiding eye contact. Within two weeks of uneventful arrivals and departures, you'll notice a dramatic difference in your dog's composure when you walk through the door.

Exercise, play and train daily but never within 15 minutes of arrival. If you come home for lunch to exercise, do noninteractive aerobics like jogging or biking on leash.

3. Teach the Wait command.

Do you have complete control when you open a door and your dog sees people on the other side? If he always listens to the Wait command, no matter how inviting the distraction on the other side of the door, you'll no longer have to worry about, yell at, plead with or restrain your dog around guests.

4. Prioritize.

The Down-Stay is the most difficult command to enforce with an excited dog, so don't try. Instead, first perfect the Wait, then eliminate jumping up with a toss of the shaker can, next correct barking. Now your dog is able to focus on staying Down. Truthfully, though, most trainers find that enforcing the Wait will automatically stop all nuisance behavior.

Separation Anxiety

Overly dependent dogs exhibit frantic misbehavior out of the frustration of being separated. Continual barking, whining and howling, destruction of his living space and attempts to escape by chewing, digging and jumping over fences and out of windows are common responses to separation. In addition to causing extensive, costly damage, many dogs injure themselves, oblivious to the physical discomfort of raw, bleeding gums and paws, laryngitis, broken teeth, self-mutilation through chewing and licking, and broken limbs from jumping out of windows.

After-the-fact corrections will confuse a dog with this problem and increase anxiety. Consoling tones and gentle petting will only embed the neurosis. Instead, provide regular, vigorous exercise and teach reliable obedience so you can give commands to prevent him from practicing his neurosis. Always ignore your dog as you leave and return, because lack of concern about separations is contagious. Also, practice exercises to directly increase his tolerance for separations:

Tying the dog in new areas, insisting he be quiet.

Out of sight Sit-Stays.

Whirling Dervish Departures—Rush from room to room grabbing your keys, briefcase, jacket, lunch box, etc. Zoom out the door and down the driveway, motor around the block, pull back in the garage and saunter into the house. Completely ignore your dog as you put your keys, jacket and paraphernalia away. Relax for a few minutes, then repeat the frenzied departure and relaxed arrival several times over an hour. Continue desensitizing your dog to comings and goings by repeating the pattern three times the first week, then once a week for a month.

Always confine your dog in a quiet area and create "white" noise with a fan, or play radio static at low volume to eliminate agitating noise created by neighbors or delivery people. In spite of every precaution to avoid upset, separation problems periodically return, so memorize and apply these guidelines as needed.

Submissive Urination

Some puppies and even grown dogs are prone to emotional states in which they either unconsciously or uncontrollably leak urine. If the dog has been given a clean bill of health by a veterinarian but wets when he greets people or is disciplined, he isn't having a house-training problem. You can't correct this problem, but you can gradually extinguish it by:

Teaching commands so you can give orders that force your dog to focus on his responsibilities instead of emotions.

Keeping the dog leashed to enable nonemotional correction of misbehaviors.

Avoiding eye contact, talking and touching during emotional episodes.

Practicing uneventful, calm arrivals and departures.

Not yelling, striking or getting angry.

Interact with aloofness with the worst offenders. Only initiate a superficial, brief pat, word or eye contact when the dog's bladder is empty. When he consistently responds well, test his control after he has had water.

Gradually try a warmer approach, but be ready to turn off the affection and issue a command if such an approach triggers a return to the previous behavior.

Good Manners on the Go

Trouble-Free Car Rides

Good car-riding manners ensure safety for both dog and driver. Movement and noise are a distraction to the driver and can obstruct the driver's view. Dogs who lean their heads out of car windows expose their eyes to injury or, if the driver swerves or brakes abruptly, are likely to fall out of the car. Contain your dog in a small space by crating or tying to a seatbelt with a short leash during car rides. The dog is unlikely to develop bad habits like barking and lunging, he'll be unable to move from seat to seat or lean his head out the window, and, in the unfortunate event you have an accident, he'll be protected from being thrown about the car or escaping out a broken window and running into traffic. You'll also appreciate the additional benefit of not having to clean nose prints from your car windows.

Veterinary, Groomer and Kennel Visits

Ensure your dog has pleasant experiences and is under control by using outings as an excuse to test obedience. Control him in the car, invite him out, insist on nice walking manners, enforce commands in the building, hand him over to caretakers without fanfare and expect composure when he is given back to you. He'll be more relaxed, and his helpers will delight in caring for their willing customer.

Begging, Stealing, Scavenging

Dogs can't miss what they've never had, so please, if you want your dog to be fit and content:

For the safety of your dog and to prevent
potentially hazardous movement and nose-
smudged windows, tie or crate him during
any motor trip regardless of length.

Feed him only dog food in his dish.

Don't look at the dog when you eat.

Keep garbage out of reach.

If you want your dog to Down-Stay during your meals, teach the
Down.

Tie the dog away from the table during mealtimes for two months.

Enforce the Down-Stay while tied for one month.

Close cabinets and closets, and put laundry away.

Never correct stealing after the fact. On discovering the misbehavior, leash your dog, invite him to make the same mistake and correct.

When using a shaker can to startle a dog in the midst of some undesirable behavior, don't let him see you throw it. Aim to hit, don't let the dog see you pick up the can, and have extras ready if one throw doesn't get the message across.

Even if you could catch the canine thief, he may refuse to surrender his stolen treasure by clenching his teeth around it or biting your hand.

Though he holds the ball, you can hold the cards. Change the thieving dog's focus by enforcing commands such as "Down" and "Come." If he is still holding the ball while responding to your commands, command him to "Down" and "Drop it." This exercise will immediately reduce a dog's possessiveness. If repeated, it will permanently eliminate the tendency.

Greatest House-Training Myths

Some dogs virtually house-train themselves, but their owners usually take the credit and are astounded anyone could have difficulty with the task. If your dog isn't a natural, you needn't be discouraged. Dogs house-train at different rates, and many won't be completely trustworthy for perhaps a year. Any dog can be reliably house-trained, if you refuse to be a victim of misconceptions.

The longer a dog is outside, the less likely he is to soil in the house. FALSE.

Dogs enjoy playing, observing and investigating and often forget about the "basics" when left alone outdoors. Therefore:

- Teach your dog to eliminate on command by chanting a phrase like "potty hurry" when he is sniffing, circling and performing. After a week, you'll be able to chant to encourage elimination.

- Always supervise toilet breaks so you'll know not to allow freedom in the house if he has not yet eliminated.

- Have your dog earn playtime outdoors by eliminating first and playing afterward.

If he has eliminated, it must be safe to give him freedom. FALSE.

Sometimes puppies and mature dogs will have to relieve themselves several times in a short period for no apparent reason. Even if he's unlikely to soil the house, supervision of an untrained dog is crucial to prevent garbage raiding, laundry stealing, counter jumping or furniture chewing.

Once house-trained, ALWAYS house-trained. FALSE.

Certain conditions can cause very reliable dogs to backslide:

Changes in diet disrupt normal elimination patterns.

Weather changes (too hot, cold, wet; noisy thunderstorms) make outings undesirable.

New environments (vacation homes, new house, friend's house) may appear to be an extension of his toilet area rather than his living quarters.

Medications like corticosteroids, conditions such as the onset of mating can cause more frequent elimination.

Dogs who don't eliminate in their crate when confined at night or for long periods are well on their way to being house-trained. FALSE.

Metabolism slows down with inactivity, so even a totally untrained dog may not soil for 6 to 12 hours when crated. Training is complete when the dog understands it is okay to move about, explore *and* eliminate outdoors, but he must "hold it" as he moves about and explores indoors.

Always scold when you see him eliminate indoors. FALSE.

Some dogs leak (urinate submissively due to an emotional reflex) when they get excited or frightened. Some dogs get frantic when left alone (separation anxiety) and soil. To stop the inappropriate elimination:

a. Teach the submissive wetter to concentrate on something other than his emotions (by giving commands in an unemotional way).

b. Address the separation anxiety by teaching the dog to walk in and out of enclosures on command, obeying a Sit-Stay when you are out of sight and treating all arrivals and departures as non-events.

Dogs should indicate when they need to eliminate. FALSE.
Dogs often indicate when they want to go outdoors and play, instead of when they need to eliminate. Also, many dogs will indicate frequently and always eliminate. If your dog demands frequent outings and you happen to be unavailable to accommodate him instantly, he may *have* to "go" because he hasn't developed the capacity and control to hold it.

Don't encourage a young puppy to indicate. Instead, train your puppy to control elimination with supervision, proper diet and a reasonable schedule of "toilet breaks." After he's developed self-control and understands the difference between indoors and outside, you can easily encourage him to let you know. But why would you need to?

The Good Dog Inside

I was once shopping with a friend, and we both stopped to look at a mannequin. My friend pointed out the belt and said, "What an ugly belt." I laughed and said, "I own one exactly like it and wear it with everything!" The adage "One man's trash is another man's treasure" applies to dogs as well as objects. Often one family member will love a particular canine characteristic and another will detest it, proving good and bad are totally in the eye of the beholder. Many dogs are given a one-way ticket to the shelter when their frustrated owners believe their differences are irreconcilable. The right perspective will enable you to channel characteristics so they are helpful instead of annoying.

Dogs were bred to do different jobs like guarding, herding, sled pulling and lap sitting. These jobs require specific characteristics to make teaching certain skills easier. Unfortunately, you may happen to own a Labrador Retriever who is never going to be required to dive into an ice-covered pond to retrieve ducks but who uses that kind of energy, force, stamina and drive to greet your guests. This type of dog not only is very responsive to structured training for control around guests, but also has the potential to learn a supercharged, unfailingly reliable recall, if given the right motivation.

Good training and unlimited love are the keys to release the "Good Dog Inside."

EMPOWERING THOUGHTS

Fear not and ignore disparaging remarks about your breed's tendencies—Shelties don't have to bark excessively, Huskies can obey off leash and Bichons can be house-trained. No breed has a patent on problems. Good or bad behavior can be taught to all. Compile a list of your dog's characteristics, and see virtues in all so they work for you instead of against you. Do any of these terms describe his temperament?

vigorous, tough, stubborn, aggressive, focused, confident, sassy, eager, fast moving, active, energetic, hyper, unyielding, spunky, clever, uninhibited, playful, curious, clownlike, affectionate, aloof, bashful, soft, lazy, apprehensive, dumb, cautious

Review your list and use new terms for less desirable behaviors. Describe him as determined versus stubborn, diligent versus willful, enthusiastic versus hyper, affectionate versus pesky. Behaviors like biting are definitely bad, but recognizing the characteristics behind them will allow you to channel that tendency into a good behavior. For instance, a reactive, alert dog is very responsive to learning commands but is also easily triggered into biting when left unattended with children who normally shriek and move abruptly.

Just like people, dogs can exhibit very opposite traits from one moment to the next as circumstances change. I have a wonderful friend who is a combination of extreme stubbornness and profound sensitivity. Melissa will belabor a point with unwavering conviction. If someone disagrees, as long as they hear her out then calmly express their view, Melissa is willing to accept an opposite opinion presented in a nonthreatening way. Likewise, as a dog's perceptions or surroundings change, so will his behavior. The dog who contentedly accepts grooming one moment may try bailing off the table the next. Always be ready to replace the unacceptable reactions as various facets of his personality emerge.

Time to Behave

Most dogs are perfectly adorable and delightful to be near at certain times. In class, my students are often awed by their dog's good behavior. "Why doesn't he do that at home?" they wonder. He is behaving because he was properly trained to do so in class. Unfortunately, some students fail to use the same logical approach of developing absolute expectations, communicating in the dog's language and following a step-by-step plan to mold the dog's behavior at home. The owner who continues to allow bad behavior at home will naturally keep experiencing the same behavior from the dog.

Intolerance Plus Love Equals Solutions

Love alone cannot improve behavior. Conversely, problems are never solved by being angry with your dog for misbehaving. Many years ago a concerned wife contacted me to help alleviate the fears of their family dog. Dealing with canine fears was easy, but I was inept at handling dog-hating humans.

The domineering husband happened to be a zoo veterinarian who disliked his very nice, but unschooled Bernese Mountain Dog. Each time Alpine heard the doctor approach, he got nervous and ran for cover, scrambling down the hardwood floor into the dining room. Alpine's past was sketchy, but it probably developed in his original home. He left that home at age one, because the owners divorced. There, he was probably mistreated by the husband. Although Alpine was never physically abused in his second home, the climate of tension and the husband's irritation and loud reaction to Alpine's nervousness fueled a never-ending cycle of uneasiness that engulfed the household. I knew change had to begin with the doctor. Though the skittish behavior was unacceptable, surprise and outrage over the predictable trait only worsened the problem. The vet needed to expect and tolerate the Bernese's fearfulness during the confidence-building stage. The doctor, however, refused to temporarily accept the problem while Alpine learned to respond to commands given to stop the scrambling so he would earn praise and replace the phobic scurrying with praiseworthy obedience.

Sadly, the vet saw nothing likable about the intelligent, responsive teddy bear of a dog. A treasure chest of splendid behavior awaited discovery, but the man refused to open the lid.

If given the chance to learn commands, Alpine's phobic scurrying could be curtailed with immediate enforcement of a "sit" or "down," once Alpine learned to expect commands instead.

CHAPTER 8

Oops! The Art of Making the Most of Mistakes

All good dog trainers value mistakes. Take Charlie, the New York choreographer, who wanted teach his Jag terrier an area Stay. While working with his dancers, Charlie wanted Pepper to stay out of the way. Crating or tying would be an easy solution, but Charlie loved difficult, detailed assignments and chose to teach Pepper to remain on a large rug when so commanded.

Pepper was proficient at the Wait at the door, and although he was only ten months old, responded to all commands off leash even around distractions. We met at a park for his first area Stay lesson, placed a rug on the grass, commanded him to "Wait," then proceeded to provide interesting distractions to see if he would break his boundary. Sure enough, he eagerly ran off the rug the first time we threw a toy. Charlie promptly returned him to the area. Pepper hesitantly crawled off the rug the second time we tempted him. After replacement, we tossed cookies just out of his reach and he wavered, then gave in to his taste buds by jumping off. Charlie plopped him back on the rug and praised Pepper each time he showed reserve. Finally, we began to think his understanding was absolute, but eventually he turned and tried to sneak off the back way.

FOUR STAGES OF LEARNING

Another owner might have thought his dog was stubborn for making so many attempts to leave the rug, but Charlie understood the four distinct phases of learning. In the first phase, the same mistake is made repeatedly. For example, when teaching the Sit, many dogs will lie down. When pulled up, they immediately sink back down again. Instead of diligently teaching the difference between Sit and Down, the frustrated owner will give up, allowing the dog to lie down and act helpless. Intangible but priceless rewards await the trainer or owner who insists on teaching the difference between Sit and Down. Respect, understanding and confidence in one's ability to teach and in the dog's ability to learn are developed.

In the second phase of learning, dogs explore a variety of options. On the Sit, the dog might lie down the first time, and when his trainer stops that, the dog may stand, jump, bite, throw his paws around the leash, or back up, thinking the point of this Sit command is figuring out the right way to avoid the position. A good trainer curtails every attempted wrong option swiftly, calmly and pleasantly until the dog realizes he is only allowed one option when told to sit.

Flawless obedience during training sessions signals the beginning of the third learning phase—selective obedience. It is now that the trainer shows "Sit" means "Sit" whether in the backyard, at the vet's office, on the street or when company arrives. If commands are enforced only in certain situations, most dogs will naturally assume that if they chose the right TIME to act differently (in human terms—misbehave), it's okay.

Just suppose that while unloading groceries you command your dog to sit as he tries to jump in the car. Suppose your son appears at that moment, so you ask him to take the dog away. You were preoccupied and didn't follow through on your request, because there was an easier way to handle the situation. Unfortunately, you just taught your dog a lesson in disobedience.

Four Stages of Learning

Recognize, appreciate and feel proud of the new understanding your dog has gained, but understand reliability must still be taught. Issue and prepare to enforce commands in the yard, house, field, street, veterinarian's office, grooming shop, on cold, wet, or hard, bumpy surfaces or while you're on the phone, with the kids, reading the paper, unlocking the car, standing on a ladder, hanging up a coat or entertaining guests.

In the fourth stage of learning, dogs normally obey commands in any setting. Still, no matter how well trained, dogs are never perfect. Experienced trainers know that even the best dogs occasionally need checks and reminders just like people. For lasting success, regard mistakes as an opportunity, not an inconvenience.

Index

ISBN 0-87605-778-4